BRIGHT IDEA BOOKS

AMAZING HUMAN FEATS OF Endurance

by Haley S. Johnson

raintree

a Capstone company — publishers for children

Raintree is an imprint of Capstone Global Library Limited, a company incorporated in England and Wales having its registered office at 264 Banbury Road, Oxford, OX2 7DY – Registered company number: 6695582

www.raintree.co.uk
myorders@raintree.co.uk

Edited by Meg Gaertner
Designed by Becky Daum
Production by Craig Hinton
Originated by Capstone Global Library Ltd
Printed and bound in India

ISBN 978 1 4747 7519 9   ISBN 978 1 4747 7343 0
22 21 20 19 18   23 22 21 20 19
10 9 8 7 6 5 4 3 2 1   10 9 8 7 6 5 4 3 2 1

British Library Cataloguing in Publication Data
A full catalogue record for this book is available from the British Library.

Acknowledgements
We would like to thank the following for permission to reproduce photographs: AP Images: Hannibal Hanschke/picture-alliance/dpa, 16–17; Getty Images: John van Hasselt/Corbis Historical, 14–15, Walter Michot/Miami Herald/MCT/Tribune News Service, 7; NASA: JSC/NASA, 25, 26–27; Shutterstock: Africa Studio, 30–31, Chuck Wagner, 10–11, Dominik Michalek, 5, 28, Joshua Rainey Photography, 23, Maridav, 8–9, Melqianbao, 13, Rena Schild, 19, Roberto Caucino, cover, Yuri Turkov, 20–21. Design Elements: iStockphoto, Red Line Editorial, and Shutterstock Images.

Every effort has been made to contact copyright holders of material reproduced in this book. Any omissions will be rectified in subsequent printings if notice is given to the publisher.

All the internet addresses (URLs) given in this book were valid at the time of going to press. However, due to the dynamic nature of the internet, some addresses may have changed, or sites may have changed or ceased to exist since publication. While the author and publisher regret any inconvenience this may cause readers, no responsibility for any such changes can be accepted by either the author or the publisher.

CONTENTS

CHAPTER 1

ENDURANCE

Some people have climbed high mountains. Other people have gone into space. A tennis match lasted for 11 hours. A woman swam 177 kilometres (110 miles) without stopping.

All of these feats took endurance.
This is the power to keep going with
something even when it is hard.

These hikers must
endure cold weather
and unsafe paths.

CHAPTER 2

GOING THE
Distance

Cuba and Florida, USA, are 177 kilometres (110 miles) apart. Diana Nyad tried to swim this distance four times. She was 28 years old on her first try. She made it on her fifth try. She was 64 years old. It took her almost 53 hours to finish. That's more than two days. Nyad stayed in the water the whole time.

Nyad proved that amazing feats take hard work.

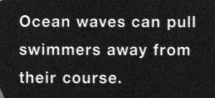

Ocean waves can pull swimmers away from their course.

ENDING EARLY

Jellyfish stings hurt Nyad on her fourth try. She had to stop swimming to stay safe.

A DANGEROUS SWIM

Sharks live in the ocean that Nyad was swimming. Nyad did not see any sharks. But she did see jellyfish. Luckily she had a special swimming costume. It kept her safe from being stung. But she was still sunburned and tired.

Fans wait for Nyad on the beach in Florida, USA.

PRACTICE MAKES PERFECT

A team of 35 people helped Nyad. But she had to swim on her own. Music helped her to focus. She trained often. She worked very hard.

She became a better swimmer. This hard work paid off when she finally made it.

CHAPTER 3

IN
Thin Air

Babu Chhiri Sherpa was a guide for mountain climbers. He led people up the world's highest mountain. He helped climbers break records on Mount Everest. Chhiri also broke many records on his own. He climbed the mountain 10 times.

Climbers spend the night at base camp before heading up Mount Everest.

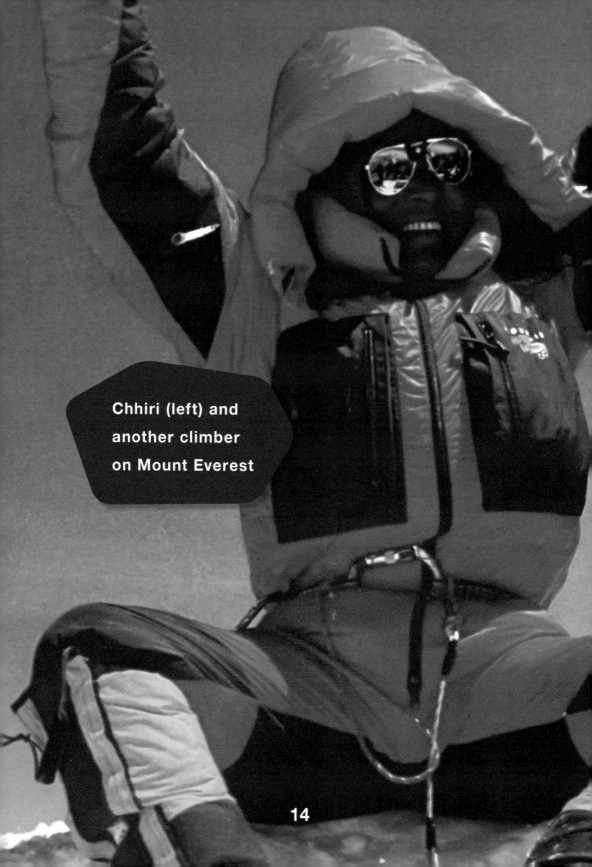

Chhiri (left) and another climber on Mount Everest

14

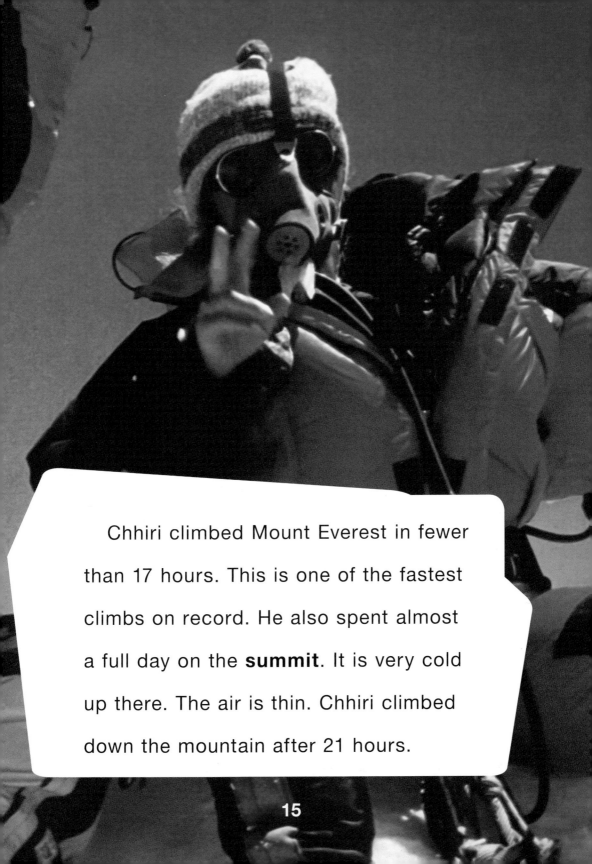

Chhiri climbed Mount Everest in fewer than 17 hours. This is one of the fastest climbs on record. He also spent almost a full day on the **summit**. It is very cold up there. The air is thin. Chhiri climbed down the mountain after 21 hours.

CHAPTER 4

YOUNG
at Heart

Johanna Quaas is the oldest **gymnast** in the world. She began competing when she was 57 years old. People are amazed when they watch her. She is better than many younger gymnasts. Quaas was still competing at the age of 91!

It takes great strength to perform on the parallel bars.

MANY SKILLS

Quaas is skilled at **handball** too. She won a tournament in 1954.

CHAPTER 5

THE LONGEST Match

John Isner and Nicolas Mahut played a tennis match in 2010. It was not a semi-final or final. It was a first round match at Wimbledon.

Neither player was expected to win the tournament. But neither player wanted to give in. People around the world watched them play.

Isner has won 13 titles in tennis.

Isner and Mahut played for more than 11 hours. This is more than four hours longer than any other match. They played 183 games. Isner won after a hard fight. He lost in the second round of the tournament. But he is remembered for not giving up.

THE LONGEST MATCH

WAS PLAYED ON NO. 18 COURT
22ND - 24TH JUNE 2010

JOHN ISNER (USA) BEAT NICOLAS MAHUT (FRA)

6-4 3-6 6-7(7-9) 7-6(7-3) 70-68

MATCH DURATION 11 HOURS 5 MINUTES

A plaque outside court 18 at the Wimbledon All England Club remembers the longest match.

CHAPTER 6

RUNNING
Hot

Dean Karnazes ran 563 kilometres (350 miles) without stopping in 2005. It took him almost 82 hours to finish the run. That's more than three days. He got tired while running. But he kept going.

People run marathons after training for a very long time.

MARATHON MANIAC

A **marathon** is 42 km (26.2 miles) long. Karnazes once ran 50 marathons in 50 days.

CHAPTER 7

SPACE
Odyssey

Peggy Whitson came back to Earth in 2017. She had been working at the International Space Station (ISS). The astronaut had been there for almost a year. Whitson had been on other space missions before that. She had done many science experiments in space.

Whitson is ready to leave the ISS for a spacewalk.

Whitson looks down on Earth.

OUT OF THIS WORLD

Whitson spent a total of 665 days in space. That's almost two years. She was the first American to spend that much time in space. She was also the first woman to do so. Whitson missed her family and friends. But she loved working at the station.

GLOSSARY

gymnast
person skilled in gymnastics who competes in exercises on uneven bars, the balance beam, parallel bars and floor routines

handball
sport in which players throw a ball to each other and try to score in the other team's goal

marathon
long-distance race in which people run 42 kilometres (26.2 miles)

summit
top of a mountain

OTHER AMAZING FEATS

- Annette Fredskov of Denmark ran 366 marathons over 365 days between 2012 and 2013. That's more than one marathon per day.

- In 2014, Pastor Zach Zehnder of Florida, USA, spoke for 58 hours and 18 minutes without stopping.

- In 1980, Minoru Yoshida did 10,507 press-ups in a row. He beat the previous record by more than 4,000 push-ups.

ACTIVITY

ENDURANCE CHALLENGES

Try these endurance challenges with your family and friends. You may need a stopwatch or a clock to keep time. You can also make up your own endurance challenges.

- Who can hop on one foot for the longest time?

- Who can do the most press-ups in a row?

- Who can keep their eyes open the longest without blinking?

FIND OUT MORE

Are you amazed by these feats of endurance and curious to find out more? Check out these resources:

Books

Extreme Athletes (Ultimate Adventurers) Charlotte Guillain (Raintree, 2014)

Guinness World Records 2019 (Guinness World Records Ltd, 2018)

Surviving Mount Everest (Surviving Extreme Sports), Blake Hoena (Raintree, 2017)

The World's Greatest Olympians (The Olympics), Michael Hurley (Raintree, 2012)

Websites

Get inspired to keep fit!
www.bbc.co.uk/sport/get-inspired

Find out more about gymnastics.
www.dkfindout.com/uk/sports/gymnastics

INDEX